www.ingramcontent.com/pod-product-compliance
Lightning Source LLC
LaVergne TN
LVHW072013060526
838200LV00059B/4665

Journeys Through the Siddur

Shabbat at Home

ISBN # 9781891662577

Copyright © 2005 Torah Aura Productions

Artwork © David Bleicher, Christine Tripp and Lane Yerkes.

Photographs: Page 3 © George Disario/CORBIS; page 7 and 29 © Najilah Feanny/CORBIS; page 20 ©Bill Ross/CORBIS; page 37 and 41 © Richard T. Notwitz/CORBIS; page 45 © Historical Picture Archives/CORBIS; page 48 © Nathan Benn/CORBIS.

All rights reserved. No part of this publication may be reproduced or transmitted in any form or by any means graphic, electronic or mechanical, including photocopying, recording or by any information storage and retrieval system, without permission in writing from the publisher.

(800) BE-Torah • (800) 238-6724 • (323) 585-7312 • fax (323) 585-0327

E-MAIL <misrad@torahaura.com> • Visit the Torah Aura website at www.torahaura.com

MANUFACTURED IN USA

שַׁבָּת

An artist cannot be continually wielding a brush.
At times, every artist must stop painting to freshen
his (or her) vision of the object, the meaning of which
the artist wishes to express on the canvas. Living is also an art. . . .

Shabbat represents those moments when we pause in our
brushwork to renew our vision of the object.

Mordecai Kaplan (adapted)

שַׁבָּת

שַׁבָּת remembers three moments in history. It remembers the creation of the world. Just as God rested on The Seventh Day of creation, we also rest on The Seventh Day. שַׁבָּת becomes a day of our own re-creation.

שַׁבָּת remembers the Exodus from Egypt. The Midrash tells us that when the Jews in Egypt were able to celebrate שַׁבָּת, that freedom was the beginning of their liberation. When we celebrate שַׁבָּת, we begin to set us free from our own Egypt-like moments.

שַׁבָּת also remembers something that has not happened yet. It remembers the future-to-come when there is peace and prosperity for everyone. Adam and Eve experienced this kind of moment when they spent שַׁבָּת in the Garden of Eden. We experience a foretaste of the עוֹלָם הַבָּא (world-to-come).

The שַׁבָּת Table

The שַׁבָּת table remembers many places, too. We remember in a midrash that God set a שַׁבָּת table for Adam and Eve in the Garden of Eden. We have a memory that Sarah and Abraham welcomed visitors to their Shabbat table. We are taught that Israel observed the שַׁבָּת for forty years in the wilderness. When we set our שַׁבָּת table we bring those moments back to life. The שַׁבָּת table also reminds us of the altar in the Temple and the Tabernacle where the priests connected the Jewish people to God. At our שַׁבָּת table we make our own connection with God.

The שַׁבָּת Seder

On Friday night there is a very short service that we do at our dinner table. It can include:

- Lighting of candles. Some families light candles at sundown. Some families wait to light candles when they sit down for שַׁבָּת dinner.
- שָׁלוֹם עֲלֵיכֶם. A song that welcomes angels to our home.
- Family blessings. Parents bless children, and then recite wishes for each other.
- קִדּוּשׁ. The prayer over wine that makes שַׁבָּת holy.
- Washing of hands.
- הַמּוֹצִיא. A blessing over bread that begins the meal.

The Emperor, the Rabbi and a Spice Called Shabbat

Antoninus was a Roman Emperor. He had a good friend named Rabbi Yehudah ha-Nasi. One Shabbat, Rabbi Yehudah prepared lunch for his friend. The food was cold because the Rabbi did not cook on Shabbat. Still, Antoninus pronounced everything "delicious."

"Mmmm" said Rabbi Yehudah, raising his eyebrows like he knew a secret but couldn't tell.

Later that week, the Emperor again went to the Rabbi's house for dinner. This time, the Rabbi served him a piping hot meal. Antoninus tasted everything.

"This meat is okay," he said to the Rabbi, "and the vegetables aren't bad, but I enjoyed the last meal you made much more. This food is missing something."

The Rabbi loved his friend and so he tried not to laugh.

"Well, something's missing," said the Emperor. "Did you forget something, or is it a secret recipe that has been handed down from one Jewish family to another, year after year after year? Come on, you can tell me. What is it?"

"Okay, my friend, you're right," replied Rabbi Yehudah. "Something is missing. But you won't find it in the pantry. You won't find it in the cellar either. You won't find it in the cabinet, in the rear or on top. You won't even find it in my box of secret recipes that have been handed down from one Jewish family to another for year after year after year."

"What's missing," continued the Rabbi, "is a spice that can't be grown, can't be mixed, can't be found or tasted anywhere. You see," he said, "what's really missing is not an ingredient at all, but the Shabbat itself."

Questions
1. What about the cold meal made it so special?
2. How can Shabbat change the taste of food?
3. How can knowing this story help us know where to point our hearts on Shabbat?

LESSON 1
הַדְלָקַת נֵרוֹת

The Midrash tells us that Sarah lit candles and baked ḥallah for שַׁבָּת. The light of her candles lasted from שַׁבָּת to שַׁבָּת. As long as her candles were lit, the cloud with the שְׁכִינָה (the part of God that can get close to us) hovered over her tent.

Every Friday night we light שַׁבָּת candles. It is traditional to light two candles—one for each of the two sets of the Ten Commandments. One is in Exodus, the other in Deuteronomy, and they present different versions of the שַׁבָּת commandment. One begins שָׁמוֹר and the other זָכוֹר, one talks about creation and the other talks about Egypt.

The Talmud calls the שַׁבָּת candles "lights of שָׁלוֹם." These candles are also connected to Proverbs 6.23: כִּי נֵר מִצְוָה וְתוֹרָה אוֹר "FOR THE COMMANDMENT IS A LAMP, AND THE TEACHING IS LIGHT." While the candles are sort of hard to explain, the simple truth is that as we light them we bring the light of Shabbat into our lives. Like Sarah, lighting candles brings God close.

Can you see the letters **צוה** in these words?
Sometimes the letter **ה** drops out in words.

מִצְוָה וְצִוָּנוּ בְּמִצְוֹתָיו

commandment = מִ**צְוָ**ה

and commanded us = וְ**צִוָּ**נוּ

with God's commandments = בְּמִ**צְוֹ**תָיו

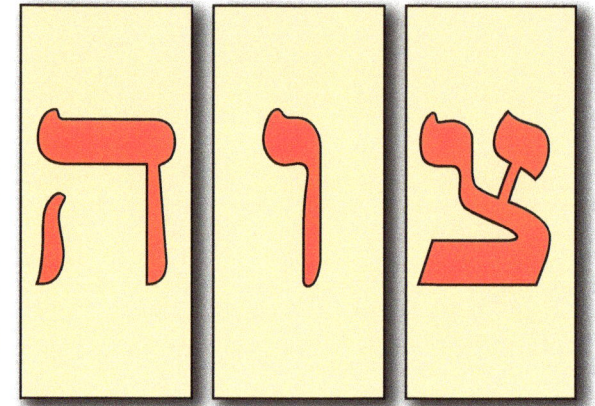

ROOT ANALYSIS

The root **צוה** means "command."

Practice these words and circle all that contain the root **צוה**.

1.	מִצְוֹת	מֶלֶךְ	מוֹשִׁיעֵנוּ	קָדוֹשׁ	צִוָּה	לָנוּ
2.	בְּרוּכִים	הַבָּאִים	מִצְוָה	תּוֹרָה	אֲשֶׁר	צַו
3.	שְׁמַע	יִשְׂרָאֵל	שָׁלוֹם	קְדוּשָׁה	מִצְוָה	קָדוֹשׁ
4.	וְצִוָּנוּ	הָעֵץ	הַגֶּפֶן	מַלְכוּתוֹ	מְזוֹנוֹת	קִדְּשָׁנוּ
5.	לְהַדְלִיק	צִוָּה	מִצְוֹת	שׁוֹמֵעַ	מְגַלֶּה	מַלְכֵּנוּ

Write in the missing letters for these words built from the root **צוה**.

6. מִצְו___ 7. מִצַ___ה 8. וְ___וָּנוּ

9. צַ___ 10. צִוָּ___ 11. בְּמִ___וֹתָיו

8

TRANSLATION

Review the vocabulary and make your best guess at the meaning of this part of a mitzvah בְּרָכָה.

    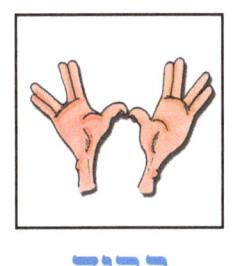

קָדוֹשׁ   עוֹלָם   מֶלֶךְ   אַתָּה   בָּרוּךְ

Take your best guess at the meaning of this text. Your teacher will help you with your translation.

בָּרוּךְ אַתָּה יי אֱלֹהֵינוּ מֶלֶךְ הָעוֹלָם
אֲשֶׁר קִדְּשָׁנוּ בְּמִצְוֹתָיו וְצִוָּנוּ

_____

_____

_____

Words

that/which = אֲשֶׁר   God's name = יי

command =    our God = אֱלֹהֵינוּ

LESSON 2

Practice these בְּרָכָה words.

1. בָּרוּךְ שַׁבָּת נֵר עַל אֲשֶׁר קִדְּשָׁנוּ לוּלָב
2. מְגִלָּה מַצָּה אַתָּה יְיָ שֶׁל חֲנֻכָּה וְצִוָּנוּ
3. עַל אֲכִילַת צִיצִית לִשְׁמֹעַ קוֹל מְזוּזָה
4. מִקְרָא בְּמִצְוֹתָיו לְהַדְלִיק לִקְבֹּעַ נְטִילַת
5. לְהִתְעַטֵּף אֱלֹהֵינוּ קִדְּשָׁנוּ הַמּוֹצִיא לֶחֶם פְּרִי

Recite these בְּרָכָה phrases.

6. בָּרוּךְ אַתָּה יְיָ אֱלֹהֵינוּ מֶלֶךְ   אֲשֶׁר קִדְּשָׁנוּ בְּמִצְוֹתָיו
7. וְצִוָּנוּ לְהַדְלִיק נֵר שֶׁל שַׁבָּת   וְצִוָּנוּ לִשְׁמֹעַ קוֹל שׁוֹפָר
8. וְצִוָּנוּ עַל אֲכִילַת מַצָּה   וְצִוָּנוּ עַל נְטִילַת לוּלָב
9. וְצִוָּנוּ עַל מִקְרָא מְגִלָּה   וְצִוָּנוּ לִקְבֹּעַ מְזוּזָה

Recite this בְּרָכָה.

בָּרוּךְ אַתָּה יְיָ אֱלֹהֵינוּ מֶלֶךְ הָעוֹלָם אֲשֶׁר קִדְּשָׁנוּ בְּמִצְוֹתָיו וְצִוָּנוּ לְהַדְלִיק נֵר שֶׁל שַׁבָּת.

TRANSLATION

The מִצְוָה of Lighting

לְהַדְלִיק

נֵר

of

שֶׁל

שַׁבָּת

חֲנֻכָּה

יוֹם

טוֹב

Most Jewish holidays begin twice, once when the candles are lit and blessed and then again when the קִדּוּשׁ is said over the wine. Both of these בְּרָכוֹת help us recognize the holiness of Shabbat or the festival and make holiness part of our experience.

Kindling (lighting) candles to mark the beginning of Shabbat or a festival and lighting the Hanukkah lights are מִצְוֹת. Each of these acts of lighting a flame is an opportunity—a chance to kindle a feeling of holiness inside ourselves.

1. בָּרוּךְ אַתָּה יי אֱלֹהֵינוּ מֶלֶךְ הָעוֹלָם
2. אֲשֶׁר קִדְּשָׁנוּ בְּמִצְוֹתָיו וְצִוָּנוּ לְהַדְלִיק נֵר שֶׁל שַׁבָּת.
3. בָּרוּךְ אַתָּה יי אֱלֹהֵינוּ מֶלֶךְ הָעוֹלָם
4. אֲשֶׁר קִדְּשָׁנוּ בְּמִצְוֹתָיו וְצִוָּנוּ לְהַדְלִיק נֵר שֶׁל חֲנֻכָּה.
5. בָּרוּךְ אַתָּה יי אֱלֹהֵינוּ מֶלֶךְ הָעוֹלָם
6. אֲשֶׁר קִדְּשָׁנוּ בְּמִצְוֹתָיו וְצִוָּנוּ לְהַדְלִיק נֵר שֶׁל יוֹם טוֹב.

My own translation of this part of the בְּרָכָה:

לְהַדְלִיק נֵר שֶׁל שַׁבָּת

_____

_____

The First Shabbat

In the beginning, God was alone. So God created the angels, the other heavenly creatures, and people, too. The first thing God created was light. It was a special kind of light—one that came directly from God. On the fourth day of creation God created the sun, the moon, and the stars. The original light was hidden away.

On the first Shabbat God stopped working and gathered all of creation. The angel of Shabbat got to sit on the throne of glory, and all of the angels got to rest. They gathered round and folded their six wings. On the seventh day they could not sing. God brought Adam and Eve up to heaven to join in the Shabbat celebration. They were the ones who began to sing, "It is good to give thanks to God," the words that later started the Shabbat psalm. The angels joined in.

God told Adam and Eve that a piece of the Garden of Eden is in every Shabbat. God said, "During Shabbat you will be able to taste the world to come." God then decided that a little bit of the original hidden light would be released into the world every Shabbat. (Assembled through the notes in Louis Ginzberg's *Legends of the Jews*).

Questions
1. What is the special connection between Shabbat and people?
2. How does Shabbat connect us to God?
3. How can knowing this story help us to point our hearts when we light candles on Shabbat?

LESSON 3

שָׁלוֹם עֲלֵיכֶם

שָׁלוֹם עֲלֵיכֶם

שָׁלוֹם עֲלֵיכֶם is the song we use to welcome **שַׁבָּת** into our home. It is based on two Talmudic stories that tell us that angels enter our home at the beginning of **שַׁבָּת**. This song welcomes the angels, invites them in, asks them for a blessing, and then bids them farewell.

שָׁלוֹם עֲלֵיכֶם can be a big family singing opportunity. It is the perfect chance for the kind of loud singing that links people together. It is also the kind of song where people link arms and sway. While we ask angels to bless us with **שָׁלוֹם** our singing can actually build **שַׁבַּת שָׁלוֹם**.

שָׁלוֹם עֲלֵיכֶם

PEACE to you	שָׁלוֹם עֲלֵיכֶם	1.
Attending angels	מַלְאֲכֵי הַשָּׁרֵת	2.
Angels who are high up	מַלְאֲכֵי עֶלְיוֹן	3.
From the Ruler, the Ruler of Rulers	מִמֶּלֶךְ מַלְכֵי הַמְּלָכִים	4.
The Holy One.	הַקָּדוֹשׁ בָּרוּךְ הוּא.	5.
COME to us in PEACE	בּוֹאֲכֶם לְשָׁלוֹם	6.
Attending angels	מַלְאֲכֵי הַשָּׁלוֹם	7.
Angels who are high up	מַלְאֲכֵי עֶלְיוֹן	8.
From the Ruler, the Ruler of Rulers	מִמֶּלֶךְ מַלְכֵי הַמְּלָכִים	9.
The Holy One.	הַקָּדוֹשׁ בָּרוּךְ הוּא.	10.
BLESS me with PEACE	בָּרְכוּנִי לְשָׁלוֹם	11.
Attending angels	מַלְאֲכֵי הַשָּׁלוֹם	12.
Angels who are high up	מַלְאֲכֵי עֶלְיוֹן	13.
From the Ruler, the Ruler of Rulers	מִמֶּלֶךְ מַלְכֵי הַמְּלָכִים	14.
The Holy One.	הַקָּדוֹשׁ בָּרוּךְ הוּא.	15.
Take your LEAVE in PEACE	צֵאתְכֶם לְשָׁלוֹם	16.
Attending angels	מַלְאֲכֵי הַשָּׁלוֹם	17.
Angels who are high up	מַלְאֲכֵי עֶלְיוֹן	18.
From the Ruler, the Ruler of Rulers	מִמֶּלֶךְ מַלְכֵי הַמְּלָכִים	19.
The Holy One.	הַקָּדוֹשׁ בָּרוּךְ הוּא.	20.

ROOT ANALYSIS

מֶלֶךְ = ruler
הַמְלָכִים = the rulers

Practice the phrases and circle all the words built from מלך.

1. יי מֶלֶךְ יי מָלָךְ יי יִמְלֹךְ   בָּרוּךְ שֵׁם כְּבוֹד מַלְכוּתוֹ לְעוֹלָם וָעֶד

2. הוֹדוּ וְהִמְלִיכוּ וְאָמְרוּ   מִמֶּלֶךְ מַלְכֵי הַמְּלָכִים הַקָּדוֹשׁ בָּרוּךְ הוּא

יְצִיאָה = going out
צֵאתְכֶם = leave

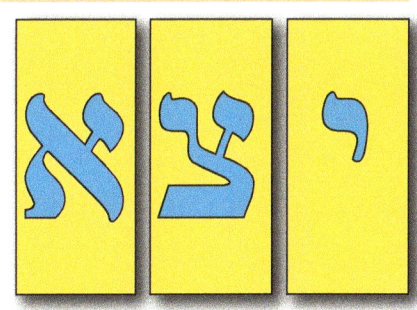

Practice the phrases and circle the words built from יצא.

3. הַמּוֹצִיא לֶחֶם מִן הָאָרֶץ   בְּצֵאת יִשְׂרָאֵל מִמִּצְרַיִם בֵּית יַעֲקֹב

4. אֲשֶׁר הוֹצֵאתִי אֶתְכֶם מֵאֶרֶץ מִצְרַיִם לִהְיוֹת לָכֶם לֵאלֹהִים

בָּרוּךְ = blessed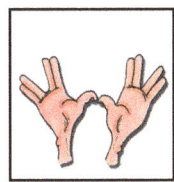
בָּרְכוּנִי = bless me

Practice the phrases and circle the words built from ברך.

5. בָּרוּךְ יי הַמְבֹרָךְ לְעוֹלָם וָעֶד   בָּרְכוּנִי לְשָׁלוֹם מַלְאֲכֵי הַשָּׁלוֹם

6. וַאֲבָרְכָה שִׁמְךָ לְעוֹלָם וָעֶד   וַאֲנַחְנוּ נְבָרֵךְ יָהּ מֵעַתָּה וְעַד עוֹלָם

TRANSLATION

קָדוֹשׁ    מֶלֶךְ   מַלְאָךְ   עַל   שָׁלוֹם

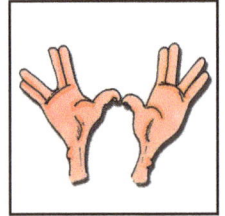

שָׁלוֹם עֲלֵיכֶם מַלְאֲכֵי הַשָּׁרֵת מַלְאֲכֵי עֶלְיוֹן
מִמֶּלֶךְ מַלְכֵי הַמְּלָכִים הַקָּדוֹשׁ בָּרוּךְ הוּא

בָּרוּךְ

My best guess at the meaning of this prayer is:

 Take your best guess at the meaning of this text. Your teacher will help you with your translation.

_____

_____

_____

Word Parts		Words
you (plural) = ■כֶם	of (plural) = ■ֵי	service = שָׁרֵת
the = ■הַ	from = מִ■	high = עֶלְיוֹן
		He = הוּא

שָׁלוֹם עֲלֵיכֶם Practice

Practice these words.

1. שָׁלוֹם מַלְאֲכֵי הַקָּדוֹשׁ מִמֶּלֶךְ מַלְכֵי בּוֹאֲכֶם

2. צֵאתְכֶם עֶלְיוֹן הַמְּלָכִים הַקָּדוֹשׁ בָּרוּךְ הוּא

3. הַשָּׁרֵת מַלְכֵי בּוֹאֲכֶם הַקָּדוֹשׁ עֶלְיוֹן צֵאתְכֶם

4. עֲלֵיכֶם מַלְכֵי מַלְאֲכֵי בָּרְכוּנִי לְשָׁלוֹם עֶלְיוֹן

Practice these phrases.

5. שָׁלוֹם עֲלֵיכֶם מַלְאֲכֵי הַשָּׁרֵת מַלְאֲכֵי עֶלְיוֹן

6. בּוֹאֲכֶם לְשָׁלוֹם מַלְאֲכֵי הַשָּׁלוֹם מַלְאֲכֵי עֶלְיוֹן

7. בָּרְכוּנִי לְשָׁלוֹם מַלְאֲכֵי הַשָּׁלוֹם מַלְאֲכֵי עֶלְיוֹן

8. צֵאתְכֶם לְשָׁלוֹם מַלְאֲכֵי הַשָּׁלוֹם מַלְאֲכֵי עֶלְיוֹן

9. מִמֶּלֶךְ מַלְכֵי הַמְּלָכִים הַקָּדוֹשׁ בָּרוּךְ הוּא

LESSON 4

The כֶם Ending

כֶם means you (plural). Match the word in the right column with its mate with the כֶם ending.

צֵאתְכֶם	נֶפֶשׁ
עֵינֵיכֶם	בּוֹא
בּוֹאֲכֶם	יְצָא
נַפְשְׁכֶם	עֵינַיִם

שָׁלוֹם עֲלֵיכֶם Practice

Practice these phrases. Remember to repeat line 2 after saying lines 3, 4 and 5.

1. שָׁלוֹם עֲלֵיכֶם מַלְאֲכֵי הַשָּׁרֵת מַלְאֲכֵי עֶלְיוֹן

2. מִמֶּלֶךְ מַלְכֵי הַמְּלָכִים הַקָּדוֹשׁ בָּרוּךְ הוּא

3. בָּרְכוּנִי לְשָׁלוֹם מַלְאֲכֵי הַשָּׁלוֹם מַלְאֲכֵי עֶלְיוֹן

4. צֵאתְכֶם לְשָׁלוֹם מַלְאֲכֵי הַשָּׁלוֹם מַלְאֲכֵי עֶלְיוֹן

5. בּוֹאֲכֶם לְשָׁלוֹם מַלְאֲכֵי הַשָּׁלוֹם מַלְאֲכֵי עֶלְיוֹן

TRANSLATION

The next three verses of שָׁלוֹם עֲלֵיכֶם are the same except for the first word.

 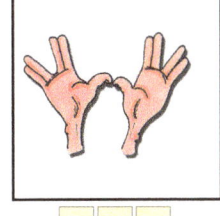   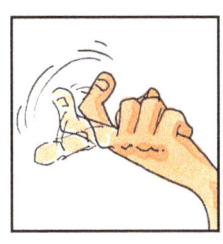

יֵצֵא   מַלְאַךְ   שָׁלוֹם   בּוֹא

בּוֹאֲכֶם לְשָׁלוֹם מַלְאֲכֵי הַשָּׁלוֹם מַלְאֲכֵי עֶלְיוֹן

בָּרְכוּנִי לְשָׁלוֹם מַלְאֲכֵי הַשָּׁלוֹם מַלְאֲכֵי עֶלְיוֹן

צֵאתְכֶם לְשָׁלוֹם מַלְאֲכֵי הַשָּׁלוֹם מַלְאֲכֵי עֶלְיוֹן

Take your best guess at the meaning of this text. Your teacher will help you with your translation.

My best guess at the meaning of this prayer is:

_____

_____

_____

_____

Word Parts

you (plural) = ∎כֶם

me = ∎נִי

of (plural) = ∎י

Words

on high = עֶלְיוֹן

The Shabbat Angels

Two angels visit Jewish homes every Friday night. When they arrive at the house they check to see if the Shabbat candles are lit, if the table is set, and if there is a sense of שְׁלוֹם-בַּיִת (family peace). They want to know if Shabbat has been "made" in this home.

If there is a feeling of Shabbat in the house, the good angel says, "May this family have a Shabbat like this every week!" and the evil angel is forced to say "Amen."

(*Shabbat* 119b).

Questions
1. What lesson can we learn from the "good angel's" blessing?
2. How can knowing this story help us to point our hearts when we sing שָׁלוֹם עֲלֵיכֶם?

LESSON 5

בִּרְכַּת מִשְׁפָּחָה

When Adam and Eve were created, God blessed them. Before he died Isaac blessed Jacob and Esau. Before she left home Rebekah's family blessed her. Jacob did the same for his children and for Joseph's sons, Ephraim and Manasseh. In the Temple the kohanim would ask God's blessing on the Families-of-Israel.

On שַׁבָּת it is a tradition for parents to bless children, husbands to bless wives, and wives to bless husbands. When we say a blessing we are asking God to make our best wishes and hopes come true for another person. Blessings are gifts from God. We ask God for those gifts for the other members of our family.

בִּרְכַּת מִשְׁפָּחָה

FOR BOYS	May God do for you	יְשִׂמְךָ אֱלֹהִים	.1
	like Ephraim and Manasseh.	כְּאֶפְרַיִם וְכִמְנַשֶּׁה.	.2
FOR GIRLS	May God do for you	יְשִׂמֵךְ אֱלֹהִים	.3
	Like Sarah, Rebekah,	כְּשָׂרָה רִבְקָה	.4
	Rachel and Leah.	רָחֵל וְלֵאָה.	.5
FOR ALL CHILDREN	May God bless you and guard you.	יְבָרֶכְךָ יי וְיִשְׁמְרֶךָ.	.6
	May God turn the Divine Face to you.	יָאֵר יי פָּנָיו אֵלֶיךָ וִיחֻנֶּךָּ.	.7
	May God lift up the Divine Face	יִשָּׂא יי פָּנָיו אֵלֶיךָ	.8
	and give you peace.	וְיָשֵׂם לְךָ שָׁלוֹם.	.9

אֵשֶׁת־חַיִל Woman of Valor

The prayer אֵשֶׁת־חַיִל praises mothers and wives for the good and important work they do. The words come from the Book of Proverbs, chapter 31. Practice part 1.

1. אֵשֶׁת־חַיִל מִי יִמְצָא, וְרָחֹק מִפְּנִינִים מִכְרָהּ.

2. בָּטַח בָּהּ לֵב בַּעְלָהּ, וְשָׁלָל לֹא יֶחְסָר.

3. גְּמָלַתְהוּ טוֹב וְלֹא־רָע, כֹּל יְמֵי חַיֶּיהָ.

4. דָּרְשָׁה צֶמֶר וּפִשְׁתִּים, וַתַּעַשׂ בְּחֵפֶץ כַּפֶּיהָ.

5. הָיְתָה כָּאֳנִיּוֹת סוֹחֵר, מִמֶּרְחָק תָּבִיא לַחְמָהּ.

6. וַתָּקָם בְּעוֹד לַיְלָה, וַתִּתֵּן טֶרֶף לְבֵיתָהּ וְחֹק לְנַעֲרֹתֶיהָ.

7. זָמְמָה שָׂדֶה וַתִּקָּחֵהוּ, מִפְּרִי כַפֶּיהָ נָטְעָה כָּרֶם.

8. חָגְרָה בְעוֹז מָתְנֶיהָ, וַתְּאַמֵּץ זְרוֹעֹתֶיהָ.

9. טָעֲמָה כִּי־טוֹב סַחְרָהּ, לֹא־יִכְבֶּה בַלַּיְלָה נֵרָהּ.

10. יָדֶיהָ שִׁלְּחָה בַכִּישׁוֹר, וְכַפֶּיהָ תָּמְכוּ פָלֶךְ.

11. כַּפָּהּ פָּרְשָׂה לֶעָנִי, וְיָדֶיהָ שִׁלְּחָה לָאֶבְיוֹן.

ROOT ANALYSIS

Can you see the three letters שמר in these words?

וְיִשְׁמְרֶךָ   שׁוֹמְרֵנוּ   שׁוֹמֵר

שׁוֹמֵר = a guard
שׁוֹמְרֵנוּ = our guard
וְיִשְׁמְרֶךָ = and he will guard you

Practice these phrases and circle all the words that contain the root שמר.

1. שָׁמוֹר וְזָכוֹר בְּדִבּוּר אֶחָד   כִּי אֵל שׁוֹמְרֵנוּ וּמַצִּילֵנוּ אָתָּה

2. וְשָׁמְרוּ בְנֵי־יִשְׂרָאֵל אֶת־הַשַּׁבָּת   יְבָרֶכְךָ יי וְיִשְׁמְרֶךָ

Can you see the three letters אוֹר in these words? Sometimes the וֹ drops out.

אוֹר יָאֵר הַמֵּאִיר

אוֹר = light
יָאֵר = He will light
הַמֵּאִיר = the One Who lights

Practice these phrases and circle all the words that contain the root אוֹר.

3. יוֹצֵר אוֹר וּבוֹרֵא חֹשֶׁךְ   הַמֵּאִיר לָאָרֶץ וְלַדָּרִים עָלֶיהָ

4. יָאֵר יי פָּנָיו אֵלֶיךָ וִיחֻנֶּךָּ   טוֹבִים מְאוֹרוֹת שֶׁבָּרָא אֱלֹהֵינוּ

TRANSLATION

Review the vocabulary and make your best guess at the meaning of בִּרְכַּת יְלָדִים.

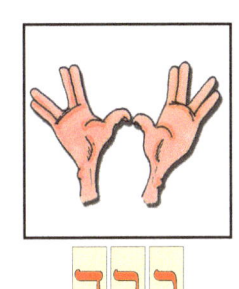

שָׁלוֹם   פָּנִים   אוֹר   שׁמר   ברך

Take your best guess at the meaning of this text. Your teacher will help you with your translation.

יְבָרֶכְךָ יי וְיִשְׁמְרֶךָ.

יָאֵר יי פָּנָיו אֵלֶיךָ וִיחֻנֶּךָּ.

יִשָּׂא יי פָּנָיו אֵלֶיךָ וְיָשֵׂם לְךָ שָׁלוֹם.

My best guess at the meaning of this prayer is:

_____

_____

_____

_____

Word Parts		Words
your = ךָ■	lift up = יִשָּׂא	to = אֶל
his = ָיו■	put = שִׂים	gracious = חֵן
and = וְ■		

25

LESSON 6

אֵשֶׁת־חַיִל Woman of Valor Part 2

Now practice part 2 of אֵשֶׁת־חַיִל.

1. לֹא־תִירָא לְבֵיתָהּ מִשָּׁלֶג, כִּי כָל־בֵּיתָהּ לָבֻשׁ שָׁנִים.

2. מַרְבַדִּים עָשְׂתָה־לָּהּ, שֵׁשׁ וְאַרְגָּמָן לְבוּשָׁהּ.

3. נוֹדָע בַּשְּׁעָרִים בַּעְלָהּ, בְּשִׁבְתּוֹ עִם־זִקְנֵי־אָרֶץ.

4. סָדִין עָשְׂתָה וַתִּמְכֹּר, וַחֲגוֹר נָתְנָה לַכְּנַעֲנִי.

5. עֹז וְהָדָר לְבוּשָׁהּ, וַתִּשְׂחַק לְיוֹם אַחֲרוֹן.

6. פִּיהָ פָּתְחָה בְחָכְמָה, וְתוֹרַת חֶסֶד עַל־לְשׁוֹנָהּ.

7. צוֹפִיָּה הֲלִיכוֹת בֵּיתָהּ, וְלֶחֶם עַצְלוּת לֹא תֹאכֵל.

8. קָמוּ בָנֶיהָ וַיְאַשְּׁרוּהָ, בַּעְלָהּ וַיְהַלְלָהּ.

9. רַבּוֹת בָּנוֹת עָשׂוּ חָיִל, וְאַתְּ עָלִית עַל־כֻּלָּנָה.

10. שֶׁקֶר הַחֵן וְהֶבֶל הַיֹּפִי, אִשָּׁה יִרְאַת־יי הִיא תִתְהַלָּל.

11. תְּנוּ־לָהּ מִפְּרִי יָדֶיהָ, וִיהַלְלוּהָ בַשְּׁעָרִים מַעֲשֶׂיהָ.

TRANSLATION

Review the vocabulary and make your best guess at the meaning of this part of בִּרְכַּת יְלָדִים.

Take your best guess at the meaning of this text. Your teacher will help you with your translation.

יְשִׂימְךָ אֱלֹהִים כְּאֶפְרַיִם וְכִמְנַשֶּׁה.

יְשִׂימֵךְ אֱלֹהִים כְּשָׂרָה רִבְקָה רָחֵל וְלֵאָה.

My best guess at the meaning of this prayer is:

_____
_____
_____
_____
_____

Word Parts		Words	
your = ◼ךָ		put = שִׂים	
like = כְּ◼		God = אֱלֹהִים	
and = וְ◼			

Being a Blessing

In the Torah God told Abraham, "I will bless thee." Then God said, "And you shall be a blessing." The Midrash explains the meaning of the added blessing.

Rabbi Eliezer said: "The Holy One said to Abraham: 'From the time when I created the world until this moment, it was I, alone, who blessed all My creatures. From now on you have the power to bless whomever you want.'"

Isaac, in his turn, blessed Jacob and Jacob blessed the twelve tribes.

"From now on," the Holy One said, "these blessings are entrusted to you—that is how you will be a blessing." And that is why parents bless their children every Shabbat. (Numbers Rabbah 11.2)

Questions
1. What does it mean to be a blessing?
2. How can one person bless another?
3. How can knowing this story help us to point our hearts when we say בִּרְכַּת מִשְׁפָּחָה?

LESSON 7

קִדּוּשׁ

The קִדּוּשׁ is a prayer that welcomes the holiness of שַׁבָּת or a holiday. The קִדּוּשׁ is actually made up of two בְּרָכוֹת. One is the בְּרָכָה that is said over the wine, grape juice, or other liquid (anything except water). The other is a בְּרָכָה over שַׁבָּת (or the holiday).

The Talmud tells us that we have to say the wine בְּרָכָה before the בְּרָכָה for שַׁבָּת. The Talmud compares the wine בְּרָכָה to a friend we see every day and the בְּרָכָה over שַׁבָּת to a Queen. One might want to say hello to a Queen first and then realize that a friend is in the room, but that would be rude. The Talmud wants us to celebrate the everyday first and then look at the special. That is why the wine בְּרָכָה comes before the בְּרָכָה for שַׁבָּת.

The בְּרָכָה over שַׁבָּת teaches two big ideas:

- We celebrate שַׁבָּת because God created the world and then rested,
- We celebrate שַׁבָּת because we were slaves in Egypt and God liberated us.

קִדּוּשׁ

1.	בָּרוּךְ אַתָּה יי	Blessed be You, ADONAI
2.	אֱלֹהֵינוּ מֶלֶךְ הָעוֹלָם	our God, Ruler-of-the-Cosmos
3.	בּוֹרֵא פְּרִי הַגָּפֶן.	The ONE-Who-Creates the fruit of the vine.
4.	בָּרוּךְ אַתָּה יי	BLESSED are You, the Eternal
5.	אֱלֹהֵינוּ מֶלֶךְ הָעוֹלָם	our God, Ruler-of-the-Cosmos
6.	אֲשֶׁר קִדְּשָׁנוּ בְּמִצְוֹתָיו	The ONE-Who-Made us HOLY through the mitzvot
7.	וְרָצָה בָנוּ	and the ONE-Who-is pleased with us.
8.	וְשַׁבַּת קָדְשׁוֹ	And the ONE-Who-gave us the holy Shabbat
9.	בְּאַהֲבָה וּבְרָצוֹן הִנְחִילָנוּ	with love and satisfaction
10.	זִכָּרוֹן לְמַעֲשֵׂה בְרֵאשִׁית.	as a remembrance of the work of CREATION.
11.	כִּי הוּא יוֹם תְּחִלָּה	Because this is a day of BEGINNING
12.	לְמִקְרָאֵי־קֹדֶשׁ	for a HOLY TIME
13.	זֵכֶר לִיצִיאַת מִצְרָיִם.*	remembering the EXODUS from Egypt.
14.	כִּי בָנוּ בָחַרְתָּ	Because You chose us
15.	וְאוֹתָנוּ קִדַּשְׁתָּ מִכָּל הָעַמִּים	and separated us from all other peoples
16.	כִּי אֵלֵינוּ קָרָאתָ	*For You have called to us*
17.	וְאוֹתָנוּ קִדַּשְׁתָּ לַעֲבוֹדָתֶךָ	*and set us apart to serve You*
18.	וְשַׁבַּת קָדְשְׁךָ בְּאַהֲבָה וּבְרָצוֹן	and intentionally separated Shabbat with love
19.	הִנְחַלְתָּנוּ.	as our inheritance.
20.	בָּרוּךְ אַתָּה יי	Blessed be You, ADONAI
21.	מְקַדֵּשׁ הַשַׁבָּת.	The ONE-Who-Makes Shabbat HOLY.

Kol Haneshamah (Reconstructionist Siddur) replaces lines

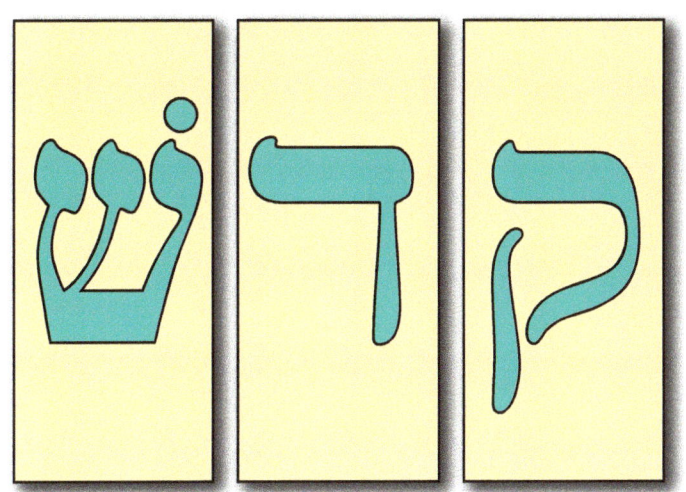

ROOT ANALYSIS

Do you remember the root קדש?
It means "holy."

קָדוֹשׁ = holy

מְקַדֵּשׁ = makes holy

קִדְּשָׁנוּ = made us holy

Practice these phrases and circle all the words built from the root קדש.

1. בָּרוּךְ אַתָּה יי הָאֵל הַקָּדוֹשׁ

2. קַדְּשֵׁנוּ בְּמִצְוֹתֶיךָ וְתֵן חֶלְקֵנוּ בְּתוֹרָתֶךָ

3. וְשַׁבַּת קָדְשׁוֹ בְּאַהֲבָה וּבְרָצוֹן הִנְחַלְתָּנוּ

4. אֲשֶׁר קִדְּשָׁנוּ בְּמִצְוֹתָיו וְרָצָה בָנוּ וְשַׁבַּת קָדְשׁוֹ בְּאַהֲבָה וּבְרָצוֹן

5. קָדוֹשׁ, קָדוֹשׁ, קָדוֹשׁ, יי צְבָאוֹת, מְלֹא כָל-הָאָרֶץ כְּבוֹדוֹ

6. אַתָּה קָדוֹשׁ וְשִׁמְךָ קָדוֹשׁ, וּקְדוֹשִׁים בְּכָל-יוֹם יְהַלְלוּךָ סֶּלָה

7. כִּי בְשֵׁם קָדְשְׁךָ הַגָּדוֹל וְהַנּוֹרָא בָּטָחְנוּ

8. נְקַדֵּשׁ אֶת שִׁמְךָ בָּעוֹלָם, כְּשֵׁם שֶׁמַּקְדִּישִׁים אוֹתוֹ בִּשְׁמֵי מָרוֹם

TRANSLATION

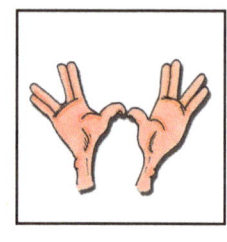    

בָּרוּךְ   אַתָּה   מֶלֶךְ   עוֹלָם   פְּרִי הַגֶּפֶן

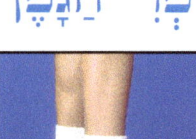

קָדוֹשׁ

שַׁבָּת

בָּרוּךְ אַתָּה יי אֱלֹהֵינוּ מֶלֶךְ הָעוֹלָם בּוֹרֵא פְּרִי הַגֶּפֶן.
בָּרוּךְ אַתָּה יי אֱלֹהֵינוּ מֶלֶךְ הָעוֹלָם
אֲשֶׁר קִדְּשָׁנוּ בְּמִצְוֹתָיו...
בָּרוּךְ אַתָּה יי מְקַדֵּשׁ הַשַּׁבָּת.

 Take your best guess at the meaning of this text. Your teacher will help you with your translation.

My best guess at the meaning of this prayer is:

_____

_____

_____

_____

Word Parts	Words
us/our = ■נוּ	creates = בּוֹרֵא
the = ■הַ	that/which/who = אֲשֶׁר
in/with = ■בְּ	His commandments = מִצְוֹתָיו

LESSON 8

ROOT ANALYSIS

The root זכר means "remember."

remembers = זוֹכֵר

remember us = זָכְרֵנוּ

remembrance = זִכָּרוֹן

Practice these phrases and circle all the words built from the root זכר.

1. בָּרוּךְ אַתָּה יְיָ אֱלֹהֵינוּ מֶלֶךְ הָעוֹלָם זוֹכֵר הַבְּרִית

2. זָכְרֵנוּ לְחַיִּים מֶלֶךְ חָפֵץ בַּחַיִּים   זִכָּרוֹן לְמַעֲשֵׂה בְרֵאשִׁית

3. וַתִּתֶּן לָנוּ יְיָ אֱלֹהֵינוּ בְּאַהֲבָה אֶת יוֹם הַזִּכָּרוֹן הַזֶּה

4. יוֹם שַׁבָּתוֹן אֵין לִשְׁכּוֹחַ, זִכְרוֹ כְּרֵיחַ הַנִּיחוֹחַ

5. כִּי הוּא יוֹם תְּחִלָּה לְמִקְרָאֵי-קֹדֶשׁ זֵכֶר לִיצִיאַת מִצְרָיִם

Write in the missing letters for these words built from the root זכר.

6. זָ__וֹ__ר

7. __ִ__ָּרוֹן

8. זָ__ְ__ֵ__נוּ

9. __ִ__ְרוֹ

10. זֵ__ֶ__

11. יִ__ְ__ֹ__ר

TRANSLATION

 Take your best guess at the meaning of this text. Your teacher will help you with your translation.

 זָכַר

 מִצְרַיִם

 יָצָא

words
מַעֲשֵׂה = makings
בְּרֵאשִׁית = creation

word parts
לְ■ = to

זִכָּרוֹן לְמַעֲשֵׂה בְרֵאשִׁית

My best guess at the meaning of this part of the prayer is:

_____

_____

זֵכֶר לִיצִיאַת מִצְרָיִם

My best guess at the meaning of this part of the prayer is:

_____

To Talk About

Look at these two phrases. The קִדּוּשׁ is built around them.

זֵכֶר לִיצִיאַת מִצְרָיִם and זִכָּרוֹן לְמַעֲשֵׂה בְרֵאשִׁית.

What is the connection between שַׁבָּת and creation? Why is שַׁבָּת a good way of remembering that God created the world? Why is remembering that God is the Creator a good reason for observing שַׁבָּת?

What is the connection between the Exodus from Egypt and שַׁבָּת? Why is שַׁבָּת a good way of celebrating the Exodus? Why is remembering the Exodus a good reason for observing שַׁבָּת?

Practice the Shabbat Afternoon קִדּוּשׁ

Practice these phrases from the Shabbat afternoon קִדּוּשׁ. What is the same and what is different from the evening version?

1. וְשָׁמְרוּ בְנֵי־יִשְׂרָאֵל אֶת־הַשַּׁבָּת

2. לַעֲשׂוֹת אֶת־הַשַּׁבָּת לְדֹרֹתָם בְּרִית עוֹלָם.

3. בֵּינִי וּבֵין בְּנֵי יִשְׂרָאֵל אוֹת הִיא לְעֹלָם

4. כִּי־שֵׁשֶׁת יָמִים עָשָׂה יְיָ אֶת־הַשָּׁמַיִם וְאֶת־הָאָרֶץ

5. וּבַיּוֹם הַשְּׁבִיעִי שָׁבַת וַיִּנָּפַשׁ.

6. עַל כֵּן בֵּרַךְ יְיָ אֶת יוֹם הַשַּׁבָּת וַיְקַדְּשֵׁהוּ.

7. בָּרוּךְ אַתָּה יְיָ אֱלֹהֵינוּ מֶלֶךְ הָעוֹלָם בּוֹרֵא פְּרִי הַגָּפֶן.

Shabbat in Egypt

Moses came and told Pharaoh to "Let my people go." Pharaoh laughed and said "No." To make matters worse, Pharaoh then told the Families-of-Israel that they had to work harder. Before they had to make mud bricks using straw that other people had cut and brought to the river's edge. Now the Jews had to make the same number of bricks every day, but they had to cut and haul their own straw. The Families-of-Israel got really mad at Moses because he had not set them free. Instead, he made things worse.

Moses went back to Pharaoh and asked, "How would you like to get twice as much work out of your slaves?" Pharaoh nodded. Moses said, "You have a choice. Kill more and more of your slaves by working them to death or give them one day a week off to recover. Then you can work them twice as hard." Pharaoh asked, "What day should it be?" Moses smiled and said, "Start on Friday night." From that day on, Israel had Shabbat in Egypt. It was their first taste of freedom (*Exodus Rabbah* 1.28).

Questions
1. What is the connection between Shabbat and Egypt?
2. How can knowing this story help you point your heart when you say the קִדּוּשׁ on Shabbat?

LESSON 10

נְטִילַת יָדַיִם

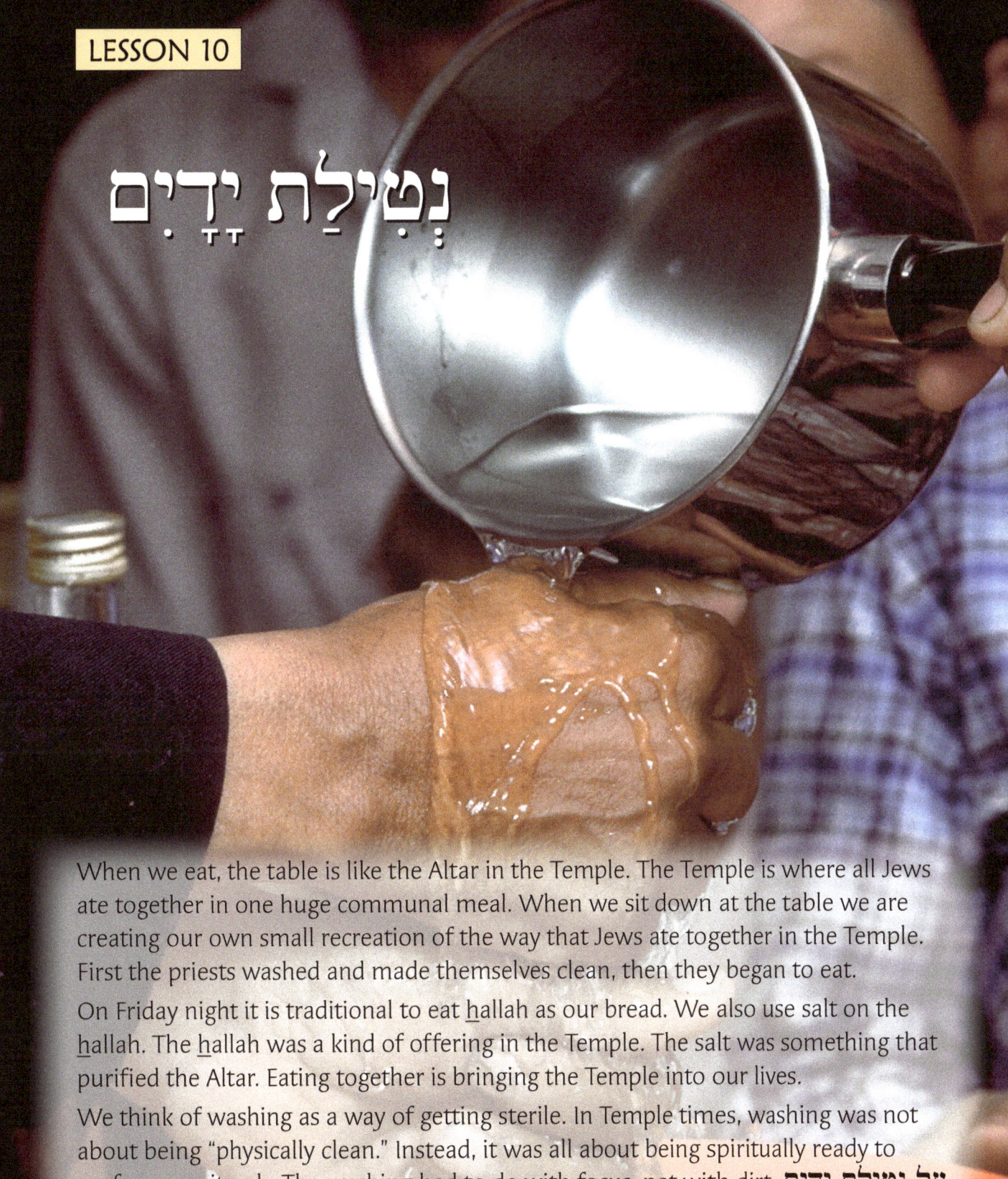

When we eat, the table is like the Altar in the Temple. The Temple is where all Jews ate together in one huge communal meal. When we sit down at the table we are creating our own small recreation of the way that Jews ate together in the Temple. First the priests washed and made themselves clean, then they began to eat.

On Friday night it is traditional to eat hallah as our bread. We also use salt on the hallah. The hallah was a kind of offering in the Temple. The salt was something that purified the Altar. Eating together is bringing the Temple into our lives.

We think of washing as a way of getting sterile. In Temple times, washing was not about being "physically clean." Instead, it was all about being spiritually ready to perform a mitzvah. The washing had to do with focus, not with dirt. עַל נְטִילַת יָדַיִם is our way of getting our heart and our mind ready for the holy process of the meal.

TRANSLATION

Review the vocabulary and make your best guess at the meaning of בִּרְכַּת יָדַיִם.

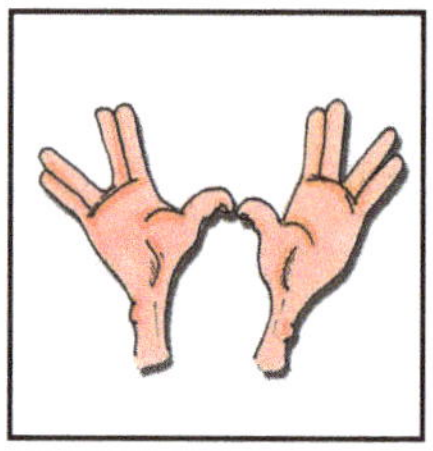

קָדוֹשׁ   עוֹלָם   מֶלֶךְ    אַתָּה   בָּרוּךְ

עַל

Take your best guess at the meaning of this text. Your teacher will help you with your translation.

בָּרוּךְ אַתָּה יי אֱלֹהֵינוּ מֶלֶךְ הָעוֹלָם
אֲשֶׁר קִדְּשָׁנוּ בְּמִצְוֹתָיו וְצִוָּנוּ
עַל נְטִילַת יָדַיִם

יָד

_____
_____
_____

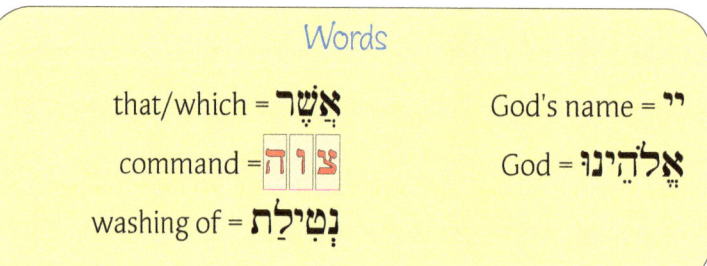

Words

that/which = אֲשֶׁר   God's name = יי

command = צוה   God = אֱלֹהֵינוּ

washing of = נְטִילַת

Moses Sees the "Afterward" of God

The Torah tells us stories of times when people felt close to God. Jacob left home to escape his brother, who was really angry with him, and to find a wife. He camped at a place called Beth El and used a rock for a pillow. Jacob had an amazing dream in which a ladder rose from earth up into the heavens. Angels were going up the ladder and angels were coming down the ladder. Different people explain the meaning of this dream in different ways. When Jacob woke up he explained his dream by saying, "God was in this place, and I didn't realize it."

Moses also left home to escape being killed. On his journey he met his wife, Tziporah, and went to work as a shepherd for her father, Yitro. One day he led his flock far into the wilderness, to a mountain that would be known in the future as Sinai. There he had an experience of being close to God. Moses was awake when he saw a bush that burned and burned but did not burn up. God spoke to him out of this amazing bush, but Moses was afraid to look.

Years passed. Moses led the Jewish people back to that same mountain, Sinai. They heard God speak the Ten Commandments and then they ignored the commandments by making a golden calf. Moses had to go up the mountain for a second time to get a new Ten Commandments. While he was up there, he asked to be able to look at God. God told him, "No one can see My face and live." Still, Moses asked again. So God told Moses to put his face into a crack in the rock. God put a hand over Moses to keep him from looking. God passed before Moses and then let him see the "afterward." Some people think that Moses saw God's back, but what the Hebrew really says is that Moses saw how things changed after God had been there. Moses saw the wake of God. A wake is the wave that appears after a boat goes by.

We are like Jacob and Moses. We want to get close to God, but that is not easy. We have to learn to realize that God is where we are—because we often forget that. And we have to learn that while we cannot see God, we can see God's "afterward." We can see the things God did. A בְּרָכָה is a way of saying that God is in this place. A בְּרָכָה is also a way of saying, "I noticed what God did, and I am thankful."

Questions

1. In what ways were Jacob and Moses alike?
2. How could Jacob not know that God was in a certain place if God was everywhere? Do you ever forget that God is where you are?
3. What things do you think Moses saw as part of God's "afterward"?
4. How can the stories of Jacob and Moses help you learn where to point your heart when you say a בְּרָכָה?

LESSON 9

הַמּוֹצִיא looks like a lie. הַמּוֹצִיא says "who brings bread out of the earth." Think about it. God doesn't bring bread out of the earth. God makes wheat and we turn wheat into bread. We combine flour, water, yeast, and sometimes other things, to make bread. It takes people (another one of God's creations) to make bread. When we say הַמּוֹצִיא we thank God for the whole system that allows bread to come out of the earth. It is the blessing that talks about the way that all the pieces work together.

הַמּוֹצִיא is not just the bread blessing—it is the whole meal blessing. When we bless God for creating bread, we bless God for creating everything we are eating. Bread becomes the symbol of our eating all the things that God gave us.

הַמּוֹצִיא

Some Basic בְּרָכוֹת

Do you know these Hebrew words? They will help you understand the בְּרָכוֹת below.

פֵּרוֹת   פְּרִי הַגֶּפֶן   לֶחֶם

מְזוֹנוֹת   עֵץ   בְּשָׂמִים

Can you figure out over what each בְּרָכָה is said? (Guessing is good.)

1. בָּרוּךְ אַתָּה יי אֱלֹהֵינוּ מֶלֶךְ הָעוֹלָם הַמּוֹצִיא לֶחֶם מִן הָאָרֶץ.

2. בָּרוּךְ אַתָּה יי אֱלֹהֵינוּ מֶלֶךְ הָעוֹלָם בּוֹרֵא פְּרִי הַגֶּפֶן.

3. בָּרוּךְ אַתָּה יי אֱלֹהֵינוּ מֶלֶךְ הָעוֹלָם בּוֹרֵא פְּרִי הָעֵץ.

4. בָּרוּךְ אַתָּה יי אֱלֹהֵינוּ מֶלֶךְ הָעוֹלָם בּוֹרֵא מִינֵי בְשָׂמִים.

5. בָּרוּךְ אַתָּה יי אֱלֹהֵינוּ מֶלֶךְ הָעוֹלָם בּוֹרֵא מִינֵי מְזוֹנוֹת.

Every בְּרָכָה begins with these words:

בָּרוּךְ אַתָּה יי אֱלֹהֵינוּ מֶלֶךְ הָעוֹלָם

Practice These Words and Phrases

Sound out these בְּרָכָה words.

1. בָּרוּךְ פְּרִי מֶלֶךְ הָעוֹלָם מִינֵי בּוֹרֵא לֶחֶם

2. הַגֶּפֶן אֱלֹהֵינוּ לֶחֶם הָאָרֶץ הָעֵץ אַתָּה פְּרִי

3. בְּשָׂמִים הַמּוֹצִיא הָאָרֶץ מִינֵי אֱלֹהֵינוּ בָּרוּךְ

Recite some phrases with these בְּרָכָה words.

4. בּוֹרֵא פְּרִי הָעֵץ   אֱלֹהֵינוּ מֶלֶךְ הָעוֹלָם   בּוֹרֵא מִינֵי

5. הַמּוֹצִיא לֶחֶם מִן הָאָרֶץ   בּוֹרֵא מִינֵי בְּשָׂמִים

6. בּוֹרֵא פְּרִי הַגֶּפֶן   בָּרוּךְ אַתָּה יי   מִן הָאָרֶץ

7. הַמּוֹצִיא לֶחֶם מִן הָאָרֶץ   אֱלֹהֵינוּ מֶלֶךְ הָעוֹלָם

8. בָּרוּךְ אַתָּה יי אֱלֹהֵינוּ מֶלֶךְ הָעוֹלָם הַמּוֹצִיא לֶחֶם מִן הָאָרֶץ

TRANSLATION

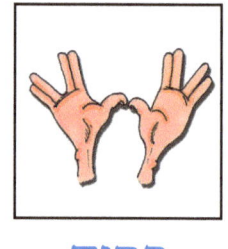    

בָּרוּךְ   אַתָּה   מֶלֶךְ   עוֹלָם   יָצָא

Take your best guess at the meaning of this text. Your teacher will help you with your translation.

בָּרוּךְ אַתָּה יי אֱלֹהֵינוּ מֶלֶךְ הָעוֹלָם
הַמּוֹצִיא לֶחֶם מִן הָאָרֶץ

לֶחֶם

My best guess at the meaning of this prayer is:

_____

_____

Benjamin the Shepherd

The Rabbis of the Talmud got into a big debate over something a shepherd named Benjamin did.

Benjamin took a loaf of bread and cut it in half. He then put meat in the middle and began to eat and enjoy the sandwich. In his joy at eating his lunch, Benjamin called out, "This is a great sandwich. Praised be the God Who created it!"

אֶרֶץ

Word Parts

God's name = יי

God = אֱלֹהֵינוּ

from = מִן

Words

us/our/we = ■נוּ

the = הַ■\הָ■

Some of the Rabbis thought that Benjamin had said a wonderful prayer, because it was based on true feelings. Two of the Rabbis, Rabbi Yosi and Rav, thought that the prayer had big problems because Benjamin didn't use the same six words that begin most בְּרָכוֹת.

Questions

1. What do you think about Benjamin the shepherd's בְּרָכָה?
2. Was it a good בְּרָכָה, or did it have problems?

LESSON 10

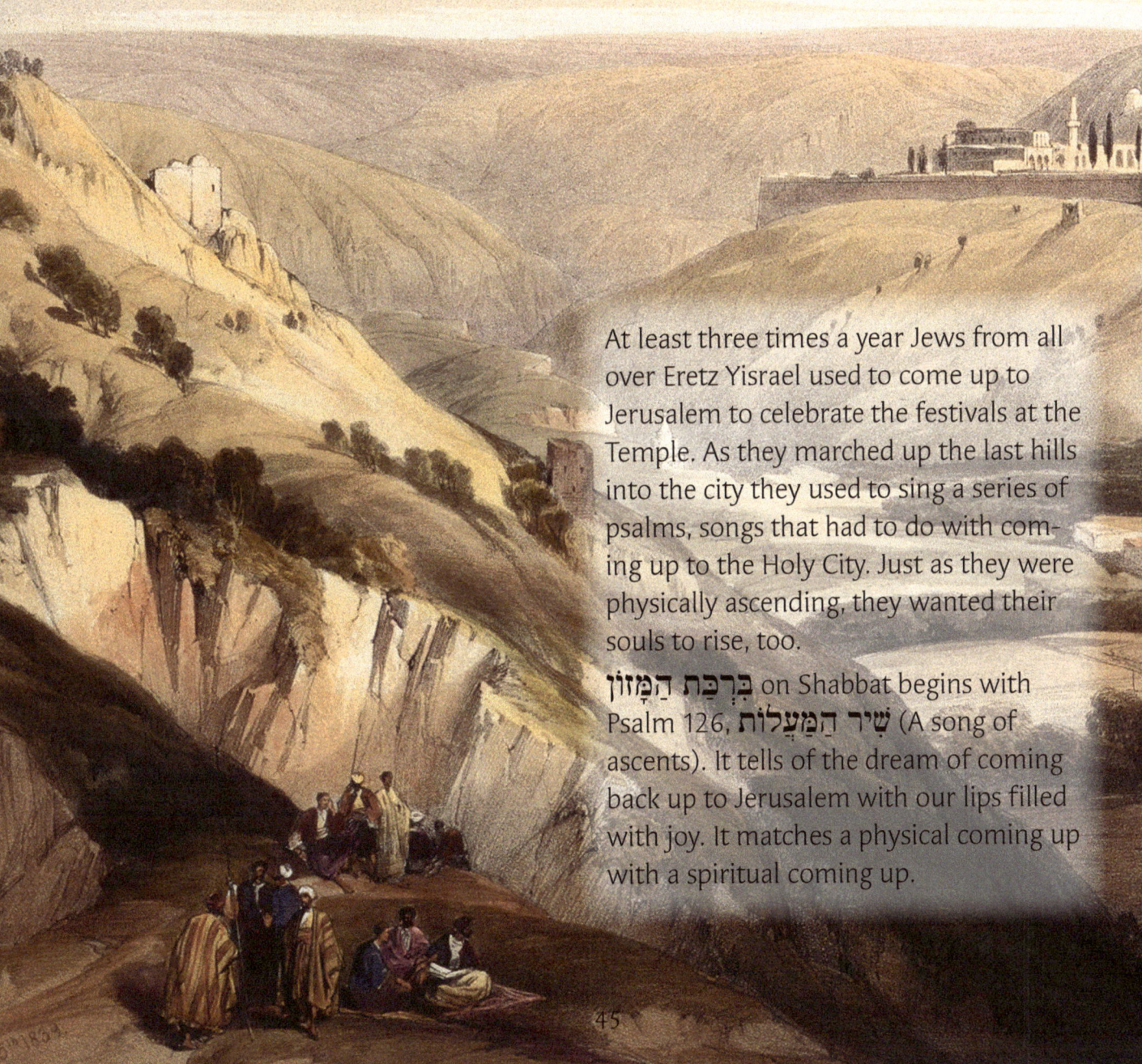

שִׁיר הַמַּעֲלוֹת

At least three times a year Jews from all over Eretz Yisrael used to come up to Jerusalem to celebrate the festivals at the Temple. As they marched up the last hills into the city they used to sing a series of psalms, songs that had to do with coming up to the Holy City. Just as they were physically ascending, they wanted their souls to rise, too.

בִּרְכַּת הַמָּזוֹן on Shabbat begins with Psalm 126, שִׁיר הַמַּעֲלוֹת (A song of ascents). It tells of the dream of coming back up to Jerusalem with our lips filled with joy. It matches a physical coming up with a spiritual coming up.

Practice the שִׁיר הַמַּעֲלוֹת

Practice Psalm 126, which is the introduction to בִּרְכַּת הַמָּזוֹן.

1. שִׁיר הַמַּעֲלוֹת בְּשׁוּב יי

2. אֶת־שִׁיבַת צִיּוֹן הָיִינוּ כְּחֹלְמִים.

3. אָז יִמָּלֵא שְׂחוֹק פִּינוּ וּלְשׁוֹנֵנוּ רִנָּה,

4. אָז יֹאמְרוּ בַגּוֹיִם,

5. הִגְדִּיל יי לַעֲשׂוֹת עִם אֵלֶּה.

6. הִגְדִּיל יי לַעֲשׂוֹת עִמָּנוּ, הָיִינוּ שְׂמֵחִים.

7. שׁוּבָה יי אֶת־שְׁבִיתֵנוּ כַּאֲפִיקִים בַּנֶּגֶב.

8. הַזֹּרְעִים בְּדִמְעָה בְּרִנָּה יִקְצֹרוּ.

9. הָלוֹךְ יֵלֵךְ וּבָכֹה נֹשֵׂא מֶשֶׁךְ־הַזָּרַע,

10. בֹּא־יָבֹא בְרִנָּה נֹשֵׂא אֲלֻמֹּתָיו.

TRANSLATION

Review the vocabulary and make your best guess at the meaning of this prayer.

Take your best guess at the meaning of this text. Your teacher will help you with your translation.

שִׁיר הַמַּעֲלוֹת בְּשׁוּב יְיָ
אֶת־שִׁיבַת צִיּוֹן הָיִינוּ כְּחֹלְמִים.

_____

_____

_____

Word Parts	Words
the = ■ַה	shows direction = אֶת
in/with = ■ְבּ	was/were = הָיָה
and = ■ְו\ו	dreamer = חוֹלֵם

LESSON 11

בִּרְכַּת הַמָּזוֹן

בִּרְכַּת הַמָּזוֹן means "the blessing of the food." It is said after eating. It is sometimes called "The Grace After Eating."

Some things to know about בִּרְכַּת הַמָּזוֹן are:

- It should be said at the table where you ate.
- When three or more people say it together, it begins with an invitation and response that is very much like the בָּרְכוּ.
- There are actually four blessings in בִּרְכַּת הַמָּזוֹן and extra pieces that one does on Shabbat and holidays (but we are only going to look at the first paragraph).
- Each of the בְּרָכוֹת tells a story, and when you put them together they retell the history of the Jewish people.

Here are the four stories:

1. Moses wrote the בְּרָכָה: *"The One-Who-Feeds all"* when God first fed Israel with manna.
2. Joshua wrote the בְּרָכָה: *"For the land and for the food"* when the people of Israel first entered the Promised Land.
3. David and Solomon wrote the בְּרָכָה: *"The One-Who-in-kindness-Rebuilds Jerusalem."* David wrote, "On Israel Your people and on Jerusalem Your city." Solomon wrote, "And on Your great and holy house".
4. The last בְּרָכָה, *"The One-Who-is-good and does good,"* was written after a small miracle made things slightly better after the defeat of Bar Kokhba. A moment of major Jewish sadness showed one good thing.

(Brakhot 48a).

When we say בִּרְכַּת הַמָּזוֹן we turn every table into a place of worship.

48

בִּרְכַּת הַמָּזוֹן

1.	בָּרוּךְ אַתָּה יי	Blessed be You ADONAI
2.	אֱלֹהֵינוּ מֶלֶךְ הָעוֹלָם	Our God, Ruler of the Cosmos
3.	הַזָּן אֶת־הָעוֹלָם כֻּלּוֹ בְּטוּבוֹ	The ONE-Who-sustains the whole cosmos with GOODNESS
4.	בְּחֵן בְּחֶסֶד וּבְרַחֲמִים.	With GRACIOUSNESS and KINDNESS and COMPASSION.
5.	הוּא נוֹתֵן לֶחֶם לְכָל־בָּשָׂר	God gives BREAD to all creatures.
6.	כִּי לְעוֹלָם חַסְדּוֹ.	God's KINDNESS endures forever.
7.	וּבְטוּבוֹ הַגָּדוֹל	Your great GOODNESS
8.	תָּמִיד לֹא חָסַר לָנוּ	has never failed us
9.	וְאַל יֶחְסַר לָנוּ מָזוֹן	Don't take FOOD away from us
10.	לְעוֹלָם וָעֶד	forever and always.
11.	בַּעֲבוּר שְׁמוֹ הַגָּדוֹל	For the sake of your great NAME
12.	כִּי הוּא אֵל זָן	Because you are the God of NOURISHMENT
13.	וּמְפַרְנֵס לַכֹּל	and You SUSTAIN all
14.	וּמֵטִיב לַכֹּל	and You are GOOD to all
15.	וּמֵכִין מָזוֹן	and you provide NOURISHMENT
16.	לְכָל־בְּרִיּוֹתָיו אֲשֶׁר בָּרָא.	to all your creatures that You CREATED.
17.	בָּרוּךְ אַתָּה יי	Praised are You, ADONAI
18.	הַזָּן אֶת־הַכֹּל.	The ONE-Who-NOURISHES all.

ROOT ANALYSIS

Do you remember this three-letter root חסד?

חֶסֶד   חַסְדֵי   חֲסָדִים

חֶסֶד = kindness
חַסְדֵי = kindness of
גְּמִילוּת חֲסָדִים =
acts of loving kindness

Practice these words and circle all the words that contain the root חסד.

1. וְזוֹכֵר חַסְדֵי אָבוֹת וְאִמָּהוֹת   כֻּלּוֹ בְּטוּבוֹ בְּחֵן בְּחֶסֶד וּבְרַחֲמִים

2. וְהַמְרַחֵם כִּי לֹא תַמּוּ חֲסָדֶיךָ   אֱלֹהִים בְּרֹב חַסְדֶּךָ

Can you see the three letters רחם in these words?

רֶחֶם   רַחֵם   הָרַחֲמָן

רֶחֶם = womb
רַחֵם = have mercy
הָרַחֲמָן = the Merciful One

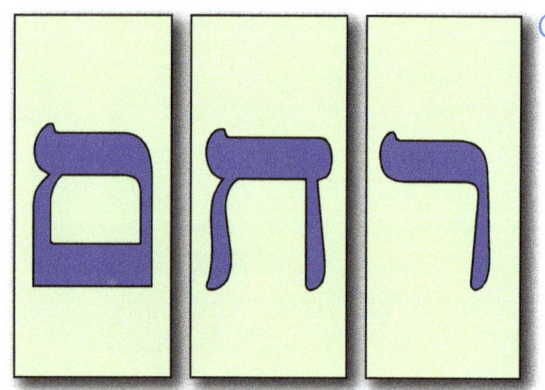

Practice these phrases and circle all the words that contain the root רחם.

3. אַב הָרַחֲמִים הֵיטִיבָה בִּרְצוֹנְךָ   יְיָ יְיָ אֵל רַחוּם וְחַנּוּן אֶרֶךְ אַפַּיִם

4. כִּי אֵל מֶלֶךְ חַנּוּן וְרַחוּם אָתָּה   רַחֵם עַל צִיּוֹן כִּי הִיא בֵּית חַיֵּינוּ

5. הָאָב הָרַחֲמָן הַמְרַחֵם רַחֵם עָלֵינוּ   וְרַחֲמָיו עַל כָּל־מַעֲשָׂיו

TRANSLATION

_____
_____
_____

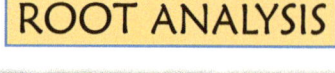

ROOT ANALYSIS

Can you see the three letters זון in these words?
Sometimes the ו drops out or becomes a י.

הַמָזוֹן   מָזוֹן   זָן

זָן = feeds
מָזוֹן = food
הַמָזוֹן = the one who feeds

Practice these phrases and circle all the words that contain the root זון.

1. בָּרוּךְ אַתָּה יי הַזָּן אֶת-הַכֹּל   וּמֵטִיב לַכֹּל וּמֵכִין מָזוֹן

2. חֹמֶר מֵזִין וְטוֹב לַבְּרִיאוּת   בּוֹרֵא מִינֵי מְזוֹנוֹת

Now practice the next part of בִּרְכַּת הַמָזוֹן.

3. נוֹדֶה לְךָ, יי אֱלֹהֵינוּ, עַל שֶׁהִנְחַלְתָּ לַאֲבוֹתֵינוּ

4. אֶרֶץ חֶמְדָּה טוֹבָה וּרְחָבָה,

5. וְעַל שֶׁהוֹצֵאתָנוּ, יי אֱלֹהֵינוּ, מֵאֶרֶץ מִצְרַיִם,

6. וּפְדִיתָנוּ מִבֵּית עֲבָדִים, וְעַל בְּרִיתְךָ שֶׁחָתַמְתָּ בִּבְשָׂרֵנוּ,

7. וְעַל תּוֹרָתְךָ שֶׁלִּמַּדְתָּנוּ, וְעַל חֻקֶּיךָ שֶׁהוֹדַעְתָּנוּ,

8. וְעַל חַיִּים חֵן וָחֶסֶד שֶׁחוֹנַנְתָּנוּ,

9. וְעַל אֲכִילַת מָזוֹן שָׁאַתָּה זָן וּמְפַרְנֵס אוֹתָנוּ תָּמִיד,

10. בְּכָל-יוֹם וּבְכָל-עֵת וּבְכָל-שָׁעָה.

TRANSLATION

Review the vocabulary and make your best guess at the meaning of this prayer.

 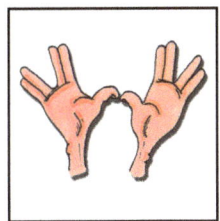  

אַתָּה   בָּרוּךְ   טוֹב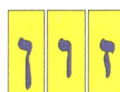

Take your best guess at the meaning of this text. Your teacher will help you with your translation.

כִּי הוּא אֵל זָן וּמְפַרְנֵס לַכֹּל
וּמֵטִיב לַכֹּל וּמֵכִין מָזוֹן
לְכָל-בְּרִיּוֹתָיו אֲשֶׁר בָּרָא.
בָּרוּךְ אַתָּה יי הַזָּן אֶת-הַכֹּל.

_____

_____

_____

Word Parts		Words
the = ■הַ	because = כִּי	prepare = מֵכִין
to = ■לְ	he (God) = הוּא	creatures = בְּרִיּוֹת
and = ■וְ\ִ	provides = מְפַרְנֵס	that = אֲשֶׁר
his (plural) = ■ָיו	all/everything = כֹּל	created = בָּרָא

53

The Twelve Loaves

In 1492 many Jews had to leave Spain because of the Spanish Inquisition. Two of them were Esperanza and her husband, the tailor, Jacobo. When they left their home in Spain they decided to go home. They went to the Land of Israel and settled in the city of Tzfat, the place that was becoming the new center for Kabbalah. Jacobo set up a tailor shop. On his first Shabbat he went to the synagogue on Shabbat morning. This Shabbat was the rabbi's sixtieth birthday. He gave a sermon about the twelve loaves of Shew Bread that the tribes put in the Temple before each Shabbat. Jacobo did not understand much of the sermon, but he did understand clearly that the rabbi said that "God liked the smell of the bread."

When he told Esperanza about the sermon she came up with an idea. She said, "I will bake twelve loaves of *pan de Dios* (the bread of God), and we will offer them as a gift of thanksgiving." When Shabbat was over, she began to bake. In the middle of the night Jacobo brought the loaves to the synagogue and left them in the ark. He said a prayer thanking God for the good things that had happened to them.
Then he went home.

A little while later the *shammas*, the man who worked for the synagogue, came in to start to get things ready for the service. He cried to God while he worked. He said, "I have not been paid in many weeks." He yelled at God, "I am doing Your work, taking care of Your house and my family is hungry. You need to do something." When he started to clean the ark he found the <u>h</u>allot and thanked God for the help.

Thirty years went by. Every week Esperanza baked <u>h</u>allah. Every week Jacobo brought it to the synagogue and thanked God. Every week God gave the *shammas* and his family food. On the rabbi's ninetieth birthday he decided to give another sermon on the Shew Bread. He stayed late on Saturday night, using the library at the back of the sanctuary to do research. When Jacobo came in, he listened to his prayer and then yelled at him, "Fool, people do not feed God." When the two of them heard the *shammas* coming, they hid. When the *shammas* took the <u>h</u>allot out of the ark, the rabbi called him a thief, saying, "That food belongs to God."

The three men were yelling at each other when the door opened. In walked the Holy Ari, the great Kabbalist, who said, "God sent me here to tell you the following. People can really share what they have with God, and with their help, God really is הַזָּן אֶת-הַכֹּל, the One-Who-feeds all."

(*From a story by Shlomo Carlbach as first heard from Art Green and then retold by the author over thirty years.*)

Questions

1. How can people share what they have with God?
2. How can God feed people?
3. How can knowing this story help you know where to point your heart when you say בִּרְכַּת הַמָּזוֹן?

LESSON 13

הַבְדָלָה

Havdalah is a way of ending Shabbat. It is a ceremony that uses a candle, a cup of wine, and a spice box. In a sense, we end Shabbat in the same ways we begin it.

Introduction: First we say a collection of verses from five different places in the Torah. These verses talk about "cup" and "light." They describe the symbols that will be used in this service. These verses also talk about the time in the future when God will help us fix and perfect the world. The end of Shabbat is a time when we hope for the best possible future.

Wine: Wine is used to welcome Shabbat. The blessing over wine is also used to organize the ending of Shabbat. Every time we use wine it is a celebration. It is traditional to fill the cup to overflowing and spill a little bit as we lift it (*Eruvim* 65a). The Rama said, "The wine shows that we are blessed" (Ch. 291, 1).

Spice: There is a tradition that on Shabbat we are given a נְשָׁמָה יְתֵרָה, an extra soul. We smell spices at the end of Shabbat to give us a boost when that extra soul is taken from us. Their smell refreshes us (Abudarham).

Fire: In the Torah we are told that one should not create fire on Shabbat. In the Talmud (*Pesahim* 53b) we are taught that God showed Adam and Eve how to create fire after the first Shabbat was over. God gave them fire as a tool. At the end of Shabbat we celebrate that gift by creating fire and saying a blessing over it.

הַבְדָלָה: The last blessing in the service is a blessing over distinctions. The Midrash teaches that Adam and Eve learned about distinctions during the first הַבְדָלָה. They saw shadow and light, and they saw the difference between holy and ordinary. We use the end of Shabbat to learn this same lesson.

הַבְדָּלָה

1.	הִנֵּה אֵל יְשׁוּעָתִי	Here is God—my SALVATION.
2.	אֶבְטַח וְלֹא אֶפְחָד.	I will TRUST and not BE AFRAID.
3.	כִּי עָזִּי וְזִמְרָת יָהּ יְיָ	ADONAI is my STRENGTH and MY GOD-SONG
4.	וַיְהִי לִי לִישׁוּעָה.	and will be my SALVATION.
5.	וּשְׁאַבְתֶּם מַיִם בְּשָׂשׂוֹן	You can draw water in JOY
6.	מִמַּעַיְנֵי הַיְשׁוּעָה.	from the WELLSPRINGS of SALVATION. (Isaiah 12.2-3)
7.	לַיְיָ הַיְשׁוּעָה	Salvation is ADONAI's
8.	עַל עַמְּךָ בִרְכָתֶךָ סֶּלָה.	for Your PEOPLE whom You BLESSED. Selah. (Psalm 3.9)
9.	יְיָ צְבָאוֹת עִמָּנוּ	ADONAI of Hosts is WITH US—
10.	מִשְׂגָּב לָנוּ אֱלֹהֵי יַעֲקֹב סֶלָה.	the God of Jacob is our FORTRESS. Selah. (Psalm 46.12)
11.	יְיָ צְבָאוֹת	ADONAI of Hosts
12.	אַשְׁרֵי אָדָם בֹּטֵחַ בָּךְ.	HAPPY are people who TRUST in You.
13.	יְיָ הוֹשִׁיעָה	ADONAI saves
14.	הַמֶּלֶךְ יַעֲנֵנוּ בְיוֹם קָרְאֵנוּ.	THE RULER Who will ANSWER us on the day that we CALL. (Psalm 84.13)
15.	לַיְּהוּדִים הָיְתָה אוֹרָה	For the Jews there was LIGHT
16.	וְשִׂמְחָה וְשָׂשֹׂן וִיקָר.	and GLADNESS and JOY and HONOR (Esther 8.16)
17.	כֵּן תִּהְיֶה לָּנוּ.	so may there be for US.
18.	כּוֹס יְשׁוּעוֹת אֶשָּׂא	I lift up the cup of SALVATION
19.	וּבְשֵׁם יְיָ אֶקְרָא.	And will call on ADONAI's NAME. (Psalm 116.13)

continued on page 58

20. Praised are You, ADONAI,	בָּרוּךְ אַתָּה יְיָ
21. our God, Ruler of the Cosmos,	אֱלֹהֵינוּ מֶלֶךְ הָעוֹלָם
22. the CREATOR-of-the-FRUIT-of-the-VINE.	בּוֹרֵא פְּרִי הַגָּפֶן.
23. Praised are You, ADONAI,	בָּרוּךְ אַתָּה יְיָ
24. our God, Ruler of the Cosmos,	אֱלֹהֵינוּ מֶלֶךְ הָעוֹלָם
25. the CREATOR-of-kinds-of-SPICES.	בּוֹרֵא מִינֵי בְשָׂמִים.
26. Praised are You, ADONAI,	בָּרוּךְ אַתָּה יְיָ
27. our God, Ruler of the Cosmos,	אֱלֹהֵינוּ מֶלֶךְ הָעוֹלָם
28. the CREATOR-of-the-LIGHTS-of-FIRE.	בּוֹרֵא מְאוֹרֵי הָאֵשׁ.
29. Praised are You, ADONAI,	בָּרוּךְ אַתָּה יְיָ
30. our God, Ruler of the Cosmos,	אֱלֹהֵינוּ מֶלֶךְ הָעוֹלָם
31. the ONE-Who-DIVIDES between HOLY and ORDINARY	הַמַּבְדִּיל בֵּין קֹדֶשׁ לְחוֹל
32. between LIGHT and DARKNESS	בֵּין אוֹר לְחֹשֶׁךְ
33. between ISRAEL and OTHER NATIONS	בֵּין יִשְׂרָאֵל לָעַמִּים*
34. between the SEVENTH DAY	בֵּין יוֹם הַשְּׁבִיעִי
35. and the SIX DAYS of CREATION	לְשֵׁשֶׁת יְמֵי הַמַּעֲשֶׂה.
36. Praised are You, ADONAI,	בָּרוּךְ אַתָּה יְיָ
37. the ONE-Who-DIVIDES between HOLY and ORDINARY.	הַמַּבְדִּיל בֵּין קֹדֶשׁ לְחוֹל.

*Kol Haneshamah (Reconstructionist Siddur) excludes line 33.

הַבְדָלָה Choreography

1. הַבְדָלָה can be made on Saturday night after three stars are in the sky. In synagogue, it is said after the end of the evening service.
2. הַבְדָלָה is usually done standing. The leader picks up the Kiddush cup in his or her right hand and spills a little wine. Often the spices are in the left hand.
3. Usually a different person is holding the candle. Sometimes it is sitting in a candle holder.
4. The opening paragraph and the בְּרָכָה over the wine are said. The wine is put down. It is not sipped at this point.
5. The spices are taken in the right hand and the בְּרָכָה over the spices is said. Then the spice box is passed around for everyone to smell.
6. The בְּרָכָה over fire is now said. A הַבְדָלָה candle must have at least two wicks. This makes it a torch. Everyone takes his or her hand, curls his or her fingers, and looks at the shadow of the fingers across the palm. We also look at the reflection of fire in the fingernails.
7. The wine cup is picked up again and the final בְּרָכָה, the one that celebrates divisions, is said. At the end of this בְּרָכָה someone drinks the wine. It is then traditional to put out the candle in some of the wine.
8. It is also traditional to hug and sway during the songs that follow.

TRANSLATION

Review the vocabulary and make your best guess at the meaning of בִּרְכוֹת הַבְדָלָה.

    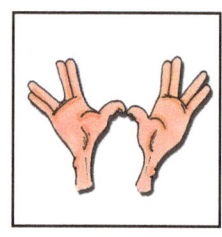

פְּרִי הַגֶפֶן   עוֹלָם   מֶלֶךְ   אַתָּה   בָּרוּךְ

בְּשָׂמִים

בָּרוּךְ אַתָּה יי אֱלֹהֵינוּ מֶלֶךְ הָעוֹלָם בּוֹרֵא פְּרִי הַגָפֶן.

בָּרוּךְ אַתָּה יי אֱלֹהֵינוּ מֶלֶךְ הָעוֹלָם בּוֹרֵא מִינֵי בְשָׂמִים.

בָּרוּךְ אַתָּה יי אֱלֹהֵינוּ מֶלֶךְ הָעוֹלָם בּוֹרֵא מְאוֹרֵי הָאֵשׁ.

אוֹר

אֵשׁ

Take your best guess at the meaning of this text. Your teacher will help you with your translation.

Word Parts	Words
the = ■הַ	create = בּוֹרֵא
	kinds of = מִינֵי

LESSON 14

Reading הַבְדָּלָה

1. הַמַּבְדִּיל בֵּין קֹדֶשׁ לְחוֹל, בֵּין אוֹר לְחֹשֶׁךְ

2. בֵּין יוֹם הַשְּׁבִיעִי לְשֵׁשֶׁת יְמֵי הַמַּעֲשֶׂה

3. הִנֵּה אֵל יְשׁוּעָתִי אֶבְטַח וְלֹא אֶפְחָד

4. לַיְּהוּדִים הָיְתָה אוֹרָה וְשִׂמְחָה וְשָׂשׂוֹן וִיקָר

5. בָּרוּךְ אַתָּה יי אֱלֹהֵינוּ מֶלֶךְ הָעוֹלָם בּוֹרֵא מְאוֹרֵי הָאֵשׁ

6. כֵּן תִּהְיֶה לָנוּ כּוֹס יְשׁוּעוֹת אֶשָּׂא וּבְשֵׁם יי אֶקְרָא

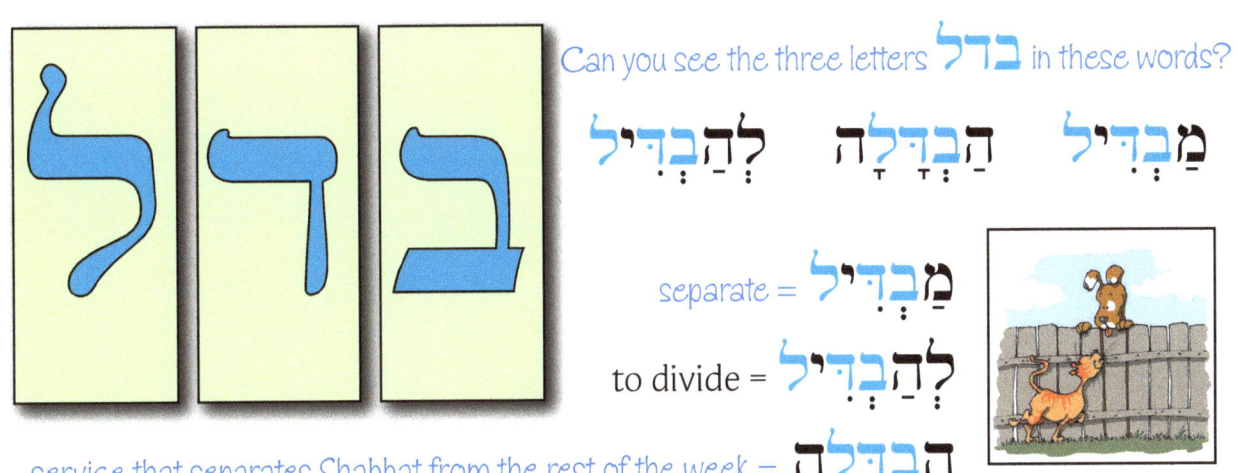

Can you see the three letters בדל in these words?

לְהַבְדִּיל   הַבְדָּלָה   מַבְדִּיל

מַבְדִּיל = separate

לְהַבְדִּיל = to divide

הַבְדָּלָה = service that separates Shabbat from the rest of the week

Song to Elijah

At the end of Havdalah we sing this song to Elijah the prophet. The song includes a hope that Elijah will bring the messiah soon.

1. אֵלִיָּהוּ הַנָּבִיא, אֵלִיָּהוּ הַתִּשְׁבִּי,

2. אֵלִיָּהוּ, אֵלִיָּהוּ,

3. אֵלִיָּהוּ הַגִּלְעָדִי.

4. בִּמְהֵרָה בְיָמֵינוּ יָבוֹא אֵלֵינוּ,

5. עִם מָשִׁיחַ בֶּן דָּוִד, עִם מָשִׁיחַ בֶּן דָּוִד.

Commentary

The concluding moments of Shabbat are a time of uncertainty. When the holiness of Shabbat fades we again begin to worry about what is to come. With the departure of the Holy Shabbat and the beginning of the work week it is important to make a distinction between the holy and the ordinary (*ArtScroll Siddur*).

Questions

1. How does one tell the difference between holy and ordinary?
2. Why is the beginning of the week an important time to make this distinction?

Adam and Eve

Adam and Eve spent their first Shabbat in the Garden of Eden. They knew that when the day was over, when night came, they would have to leave the garden. As it began to get dark they got scared. The darker it got, the more their fear grew. Adam was scared that the serpent would return and bite him in the heel. God told Adam to pick up two rocks. One rock was darkness. The other was the shadow of death. Adam banged the two rocks together, and out came a spark. The spark lit a fire, the fire lit a torch, and the torch was held high in the air, showing Adam and Eve where to go as they left the garden. Together they prayed, "בָּרוּךְ אַתָּה יי אֱלֹהֵינוּ מֶלֶךְ הָעוֹלָם בּוֹרֵא מְאוֹרֵי הָאֵשׁ," thanking God for the creation of fire. Then, as they watched the shadows flicker, they realized that God made a world with הַבְדָּלָה in it. They knew that fire could not be created on Shabbat, but now it could. They thanked God for all the distinctions, ending בָּרוּךְ אַתָּה יי הַמַּבְדִּיל בֵּין קֹדֶשׁ לְחוֹל. This was the first הַבְדָּלָה. The next day Adam and Eve began to use the fire to cook, to keep warm, and as a tool.

(From *P.R.E.* 20 and various sources cited in Ginzburg, *Legends of the Jews*)

Questions

1. Why are people scared of the dark?
2. What is it like to look into a flame or a fire?
3. What did Adam and Eve learn from the first fire?
4. How can knowing this story help you to point your heart when you participate in הַבְדָּלָה?